COPYRIGHT © 2019
ORGANICALLY DRIVEN

TABLE OF
CONTENTS

Welcome to the World of Garden Skin	1
Procedural Overview	3
Plants	5
Method of Oil Extraction	25
Methods of Formulation	27
Methods of Preservation	34

WELCOME TO THE WORLD OF
GARDEN SKIN

Hey Pretty Thing,

So you may think that you're ready to make a change; and you may feel ready to fully dive into DIY skincare… but also, you may not. You may need a little encouragement.

There are many wonderful benefits to making your own skincare products from the garden.

DON'T FEED YOUR SKIN POISON ANYMORE!

Your skin is your body's most noticeable organ. Like all organs, what goes on, goes in. Organs ingest whatever they are exposed to. Why not make this something good?

Don't spend beaucoup bucks on skincare that's filled with preservatives. The benefits of using all-natural, vegan ingredients, is not only about the glow you will experience on your external body, but it is also about the benefits you will experience on your internal body. Natural ingredients hold natural antioxidants. These antioxidants can help with how you age on the outside, and how you *feel* on the inside.

I welcome you to the exciting world of DIY products, garden-to-skin style.

It's easier than you may think. This handbook is a *simple* instructional guide, in hopes that you will find garden-made skincare, just as rewarding, as it is beneficial. This can be a lifestyle choice, not just a one-time craft experiment.

Live Well. Be Well.

Brooke

PROCEDURAL
OVERVIEW

The Overall Steps to Garden Skin

How will you acquire plants to use- in a *consistent* manner? Options:
- Research the plant properties of plants you find in your own backyard.
- Build your own skin garden.
    OD garden kits at organicallydriven.org/shop
- Use someone else's garden.
    Find a community garden or a farm, with organic plants, in your area.
- Use organic grocery store finds.

Which plants will your skin love the most? Choose them:
Read through some of our favorites in the *Plants* section.
 • Tip: If you've chosen a plant that is not listed in our *Plants* section, make sure to use an internet search the find out the safety and information on how to extract all the good stuff for your skin.

What tools will you need? Order them:
OD tool sets: organicallydriven.org/shop

Now that you have the plants, how will you extract their nutrients? Learn-by-doing:
See our *Method of Extraction* section, and give it a try!

When will this process start to be fun!? Formulate and then lavish yourself:
See our *Methods of Formulation* section in this handbook.

PLANS

ALOE VERA

Good For: inflammation, acne, and dryness

The juice inside the aloe vera plant is high in antioxidants, enzymes, and vitamins A and C. The extracted juice can be used in formulas for moisture, when used sparingly. The main benefit of this succulent, however, is its ability to calm down inflamed skin caused by a sunburn, rosacea or acne.

How to Extract:
1. Cut off the top third of the aloe vera leafs, and then the spines.
2. Slice away the skin from the top and bottom of the leaf.
3. You will see a clear slab of gel from the leaf- this is your stuff! Rinse the gel 3 times.
4. Store in a glass jar until ready for use.

Cautions:
- Always perform a patch test before using any ingredient in your products.

Recommended maximum amount per 6 oz product: 3 oz

BASIL

Good for: acne, small wounds, burns, sores

Basil is a great natural antiseptic and can be used to sting away an over-production of oil that leads to acne. It also has a soothing and relaxing effect that helps while dealing with eczema. Basil oil's anti-inflammatory properties, make it an excellent skin remedy for irritations, small wounds, sores, and even burns. Basil oil contains vitamin C, which increases skin's cell metabolism, and the rate of cell turnover, resulting in help with hyper-pigmentation. This turn-over helps to maintain the skin's collagen, which is responsible for the dermis layer and its elasticity.

How to Extract:
Steam Distillation

Cautions:
- Do not use basil oil if you are pregnant or have a seizure disorder.
- Always dilute the basil oil and use it sparingly on the skin because it can cause irritation.
- Always perform a patch test before using any ingredient in your products.

Recommended maximum amount per 6 oz product: .2 oz

CALENDULA

Good for: acne, rashes, natural product preservation

Calendula oil has anti-fungal, anti-inflammatory, and antibacterial properties that make it useful in healing wounds, soothing eczema, and relieving pain from a rash. It's also used as an antiseptic. These properties also make calendula oil a great plant to treat acne. Calendula oil has been shown to improve the overall appearance of skin by promoting skin hydration and firmness. You can try to include calendula oil to your products and use twice per day, to protect from a dermatitus rash.

How to Extract:
Steam Distillation

Cautions:
- Do not use calendula oil if you are pregnant or have a seizure disorder.
- Do not use if you will be having surgery within two weeks, due to sedative properties.
- Always perform a patch test before using any ingredient in your products.

Recommended maximum amount per 6 oz product: 1 oz

CHAMOMILE

Good for: discoloration, inflammation, sensitivity, environmental damage

Chamomile is an antibacterial, anti-fungal, anti-inflammatory and antiseptic. It is also considered to be hypoallergenic with the ability to neutralize skin irritants. Chamomile is a miracle healer and contains: bisabolol, chamazulene, and apigen. Bisabolol is responsible for anti-inflammation, anti-irritation, and is both an anti-fungal and anti-bacterial. Bisabolol is found in both German and Roman chamomile strands. German chamomile has a higher concentration of Bisabolol. Chamazulene is only found in the chamomile strands of Roman and German chamomile. When distilled, German chamomile forms a compound with matricin and causes the essential oil to turn a bright blue hue, which provides a form of chamomile extract that is particular with anti-inflammatory properties. Lastly, apigen is a flavonoid which reduces oxidative damage, that has resulted from environmental stressors. It is found in both German and Roman chamomile strands, but it is only present in the flowers.

How to Extract:
Steam Distillation

Cautions:
- Always perform a patch test before using any ingredient in your products.

Recommended maximum amount per 6 oz product: 2 oz

LAVENDER

Good for: stressed skin, detoxification, acne, aging, discoloration

Surprisingly, acne can flare up when your skin is not balanced in producing enough of its own oil, called sebum. Even dry skin can be a cause for acne when sebum production is too much due to your skin overcompensating to relieve dryness. Lavender reduces the amount of overproduced sebum that causes clogged pores and acts as a natural moisture-barrier, balancing agent. Lavender oil is perfect for preventing and also healing acne of dry skin. Lavender oil also is known to reduce redness, blotchy patches, and to help fight signs of aging that are due to environmental stressors. It is a potent source of antioxidants and other beneficial phytochemicals that fight free radical damage. The antioxidants in lavender oil can help with discoloration of dark age spots, and can prevent wrinkles and fine lines.

How to Extract:
Steam Distillation

Cautions:
- Always perform a patch test before using any ingredient in your products.

Recommended maximum amount per 6 oz product: 1 oz

LEMON BALM

Good for: problematic skin, fine lines, wrinkles

Lemon Balm soothes, cleanses, tightens the skin, and fights fine lines and wrinkles by stimulating circulation without irritation. It is also a strong antibacterial agent and helps maintain clear skin by protecting from occasional acne flare-ups, or other problematic skin conditions. Research has shown that lemon balm contains caffeic and ferulic acids which can be infused to penetrate the 3 layers of skin and protects from UV damage. Lemon Balm contains high levels of antioxidants, flavonoids, tannins, eugenol and antiviral agents. This herb can also be used for aromatic relaxation as it is known to calm over-active thinking and anxiety.

How to Extract:
Steam Distillation

Cautions:
- Always perform a patch test before using any ingredient in your products.

Recommended maximum amount per 6 oz product: .5 oz

MINT

Good for: brightening, rejuvenation, acne

Mint has strong antibacterial properties and contains salicylic acid which are wonderful in preventing acne. When applied to the skin, mint's refreshing qualities allow your skin to relax, while fighting the bacteria of any blemishes that might be present. Mint removes grime from your pores acts as a mild astringent which can be a great toning product for your skin. Mint also contains vitamin A, which controls the secretion of oil and will dry acne while cleaning out your pores. However, mint can also be a great ingredient to ward off unwanted aging. When used with certain ingredients, such as honey, mint can be a great hydrator, that will lock in moisture for continuous hydration throughout the day, keeping fine lines minimized. Mint is antioxidant-rich, with an ability to neutralize free radicals, and promote healthy blood flow, which all prevent early signs of aging.

How to Extract:
Steam Distillation

Cautions:
- Always perform a patch test before using any ingredient in your products.

  Recommended maximum amount per 6 oz product: .5 oz

ROSE

Good for: dryness, dullness

Rose contains vitamin C and vitamin E and is known to stimulate cell-turnover rate for increased collagen production. Rose is a very moisturizing ingredient, and can make your skin feel softer and more supple with just one use, just like a rose petal itself. Oil extracted from rose petals can also protect your skin against pollution, airborne irritants and trans-epidermal water loss. Rose has antiseptic properties which help restore your skin's pH levels, resulting in continuous moisture protection throughout the day. Not to mention, the lovely scent of rose can be used as an aromatic to help relax your nervous system.

How to Extract:
Steam Distillation

Cautions:
- Always perform a patch test before using any ingredient in your products.

Recommended maximum amount per 6 oz product: 2 oz

ROSEMARY

Good for: environmental damage, aging

Along with the many internal benefits of using rosemary in cooking, rosemary can work wonders in a skincare regiment. The nutrients of rosemary can help protect skin cells from damage that's often caused by the environmental stressors of the sun and free radicals. Since rosemary has natural antiseptic properties, it's a superior disinfectant for our skin and hair. In fact, this essential oil is known to promote a healthy, moisturized scalp and reverse premature graying.

How to Extract:
Steam Distillation

Cautions:
- Always perform a patch test before using any ingredient in your products.

Recommended maximum amount per 6 oz product: .8 oz

THYME

Good for: discoloration due to acne, dullness, dryness

The aromatic nature of thyme opens up pores and perks up fatigued skin, instantly. Thyme delivers anti-fungal and antiseptic properties, inhibiting surface bacteria. With its circulatory and medicinal properties, thyme fortifies the skin with its ability to repair tissue. Thyme helps ward off tightness and itching, caused by overly dry skin. Thyme is known to stimulate cell-turnover rate by increasing blood flow to skin. This perks up fatigued skin and boosts overall skin health. With the strong ability to increase circulation, scar tissue from acne or other skin injuries, will start to fade with continuous use of thyme. Acneic conditions receive incredible healing and antiseptic toning. The properties of oil extracted from thyme, maximize the overall health of skin, including acne, while preventing post-inflammation hyperpigmentation.

How to Extract:
Steam Distillation

Cautions:
- Always perform a patch test before using any ingredient in your products.

Recommended maximum amount per 6 oz product: .8 oz

METHOD OF OIL EXTRACTION

STEAM DISTILLATION METHOD

Ingredients
- Plant material

Equipment needed
- Crock pot with a lid
- Distilled water
- Fresh plant material (enough to fill the crockpot about half full)

Process

1. Place the plant material in the crock pot and cover with water. The water shouldn't fill more than ¾ of the crockpot. Put the lid on *upside down*. The concave structure will allow any steam that forms, to condense and fall back into the pot.
2. Turn the crock pot on high to heat the water. Keep crockpot on for 4 hours.
3. After the plant material is cooked, turn off and let the crockpot cool. When it is cool, place the inside of the crock pot into the refrigerator. Leave it in the refrigerator overnight.
4. The next day, pull the crock pot out of the refrigerator. A thin film of hardened oil will form on the top after cooling. These are your useful oils! Carefully lift the oil out of the water. Do This quickly because the hardened oil melts fast!
5. Once the oil has turned back into a liquid state, pour the oil into an amber glass bottle with a cap, label the bottle clearly, and store away from light and heat.

METHODS OF
FORMULATION

Now that you know some basic plant remedies and their properties, it's time to put that knowledge to use. This section is the procedural information of preferred methods to create formulas for: make-up remover, cleansers, exfoliants, serums, and moisturizing creams.

I think it's important (and exciting) to experiment on your own, and to come up with some of your own recipes, based on the plants you find in your own garden. It's always important to research these plant properties, as to ensure the plants you use will be beneficial to your current skin's state. The state of your skin will drastically improve upon using the right natural ingredients incorporated into your skincare products. Thus, it is important to adjust your routine when needed, and change the ingredients in your formulas, accordingly. However, be wary of making a formula change too quickly, as your skin does need time to adjust.

MAKE-UP REMOVER AND MOISTURIZING CREAM

Oil that's been extracted from rose petals can create a wonderful additive to any cream or make-up remover. I recommend to create a creamy product that will remove unwanted grime, effortlessly, but can double as a moisturizer to keep things simple. The following is an example of making a single product that doubles in its use, with two functions.

Here's how:
Explained Technique
Double-boil method

Ingredients
¼ cup of almond oil
2 tablespoons of coconut oil
2 tablespoons of beeswax pellets
1 tablespoon of shea butter
1 tablespoon of rose petal oil extract (optional)

Equipment and Tools:
- Pot
- Jar

Directions
1. Place the first four ingredients into a heat-safe jar.

2. Fill a pot with about 3 to 4 inches of water. Bring the water to a simmer.

3. Place the entire jar into the boiling water and let the contents melt, stirring occasionally. Do not. cover the pot or the jar.

4. Take the jar out of the water and add the rose petal extract oil (optional).

5. Transfer the mixture to a clean jar, then let it cool and harden at room temperature.

6. Close the jar, then store it in a cool, dry place.

Application: This cream is safe to use 2 times per day. It will last about 3 months.

FOAMINIG CLEANSER

I recommend creating a foaming face cleanser to use two times per day. I also recommend a liquid cleanser for sake of ease. The whole goal is to create a system that is easy to sustain, easy to repeat and easy to create. Remember, this can be a lifestyle, not just a hobby.

Here's how:
Explained Technique
Blend method

Ingredients
1/4 cup liquid castille soap
1/4 cup water
2 tsp almond oil
2 tsp aloe vera gel
2 tsp glycerin
8-12 drops of extracted oils

Equipment and tools
- Blender
- Spoon
- Foam lid container

Directions
1. Blend all the ingredients, besides the Castile soap, in a blender.

2. Add extracted oil(s) into a blender. Choose any combination of essential oils that you decided would work for you.

3. Be cognizant that the oils will change the smell of the formula. Blend.

4. Add the Castile soap to the blender and stir with a spoon.

5. Add to foam bottle. Pump, pump, ready!

Application: This cleanser is safe to use 2 times per day. It will last about 1 month.

EXFOLIANT

It's important to exfoliate your skin 1-2 times per week to ward off dead skin cells. Therefore, making a product that has a higher shelf life is important. I recommend creating a bar soap. The easiest method is melt-and-pour. Make sure to keep your bar as dry as possible between washings. I recommend using a travel bar soap container to store the product- this will help sustain its life.

Here's how:
Explained Technique
Melt-and-pour

Ingredients
Melt & pour soap base
Natural loofah
10 drops extracted oil

Equipment & Tools
- Silicon mold
- Knife
- Microwave-safe bowl
- Microwave (alternative: use a stove top)

Directions
1. Slice loofah into small rounds that will fit into your mold. Place into the mold.

2. Cut chunks of soap and place into a microwave-safe bowl. Microwave to melt on 15 second intervals until completely melted, stir between intervals.

3. Stir in selected essential oils.

4. Pour mixture into molds and cool at room temperature, until hardened (about 45 minutes).

5. Remove from molds.

Application: This exfoliant is safe to use 2 times per week. It will last about 3 months.

SERUM

Making a serum is even more simple! A serum is a mixture of highly concentrated extracts mixed together, and used to treat various skin conditions. I recommend focusing on your primary skincare concern, and then choose your formula and extracts accordingly.

Here's how:
Explained Technique
Mix

Ingredients
1 tbs base oil
(almond oil for normal skin, avocado oil for dry skin, hemp seed for oily skin)
1/2 tbs secondary oil
(rose oil for normal skin, hyaluronic acid and vitamin E for dry skin, tea tree for oily skin)
2-5 drops essential oil
(lavender oil for normal skin, thyme dry skin, lemon balm for oily skin)

Equipment and Tools
- 1 oz amber glass bottle
- Funnel

Directions
1. Use funnel to add ingredients into the amber glass bottle.

2. Dilute with water if desired; Store in refrigerator.

Application: safe to use twice a day, keep away from sunlight. Use after washing your face. Let dry before applying moisturizer.

METHODS OF
PRESERVATION

Adding a preservative to your formulations is the best way to preserve your skincare products. You may choose to opt out, as by definition, adding a preservative makes your all-organic formula, inorganic.

If you get frustrated with wasting product, due to a short shelf life, you may want to add a preservative. For the sake of keeping this handbook for those who are organically driven, here is our suggestion:

Use extracts that have anti-fungal and anti-bacterial properties.
- Chamomile
- Calendula Flowers
- Thyme

While using these in all your products, will not dramatically increase shelf life, it will help. It's extremely difficult to make organic skincare to sell commercially. It is important to keep your products as free of chemicals as possible for personal use, or to distribute to friends and family.

Photography Citations:

Cover: Catie Stanley, Photographer, Hemet, CA ©2017
Model: Brooke Gallagher

Page 2: Catie Stanley, Photographer, Hemet, CA ©2017
Model: Brooke Gallagher

Page 3, 5, 8, 9, 13, 15, 17, 21, 23, 27: Shutterstock Stock Photos ©2019

Page Intro, 11, 13, 25: Dreamstime Stock Photos ©2019

www.ingramcontent.com/pod-product-compliance
Lightning Source LLC
Chambersburg PA
CBHW060759090426
42736CB00002B/86